ORIENTAL
CARPETS

Michele Campana

ORIENTAL
CARPETS

**CASSELL
LONDON**

Cassell Publishers Limited
Artillery House, Artillery Row
London SW1P 1RT

Translated by Adeline Hartcup from the Italian original
Tappeti d'Oriente

© Gruppo Editoriale Fabbri, Bompiani, Sonzogno, Etas S.p.A., Milan 1966,
1984

This edition 1988

British Library Cataloguing in Publication Data
Campana, Michele
Oriental carpets. — (Cassell's styles in art).
1. Asian carpets
I. Title   II. Tappeti d'oriente. *English*
746.7'5

ISBN 0-304-32176-1

Printed in Italy by Gruppo Editoriale Fabbri, Milan

CONTENTS

Page

HISTORICAL AND TECHNICAL BACKGROUND

The Oriental carpet, that product of fine craftsmanship which often rises to the level of a true work of art, has very ancient origins hard to pin-point exactly in time and place. It is said, and rightly, that knowledge of Oriental carpets is hard to come by: because they are made of perishable material, tangible proofs are not always available, which is why we have to be satisfied with representations of carpets in mural paintings and bas-reliefs as evidence of their earliest origins.

It is also difficult to enter into the abstract spirit which inspires Oriental carpets and is their main theme. Understanding them means understanding the meaning of all their carefully designed motifs and shapes. The pattern is never a chance affair, or merely ornamental. Generally speaking, it is the intimate expression of a people's history, faith and civilisation;

and in particular it portrays the history, faith and civilisation of a single caste, tribe or family, and even sometimes of an individual philosopher or poet. For us in the West, it is hard indeed to grasp the spirit inspiring the design of a carpet, which to the Oriental is so intimate and jealously cherished a possession.

While carpets in the West are generally looked upon as decorations and coverings for the floor, for Orientals, rich and poor alike, they are almost their only domestic furniture. In the large reception rooms, the *talar,* carpets are used as sofas, cushions and door-hangings as well as to decorate the floor. They are laid on the doorstep to welcome all visitors to the home, and they serve as beds which are spread out at night and rolled up during the day. Most important of all there is the religious function of the carpet— quite apart from the special uses of the prayer-rug— which has been described as 'a creed in colours', and which we will speak of later.

Rare and valuable carpets are to be found in all temples and almost all religions. In ancient Egypt they were used to decorate the walls of tombs, and they were spread on the ground for the sacred bull to lie on. Before Mahomed they decorated the Káaba, and during his lifetime (AD 570–632) mosques and minarets were literally covered with them. In Buddhist temples and Christian cathedrals, too, there have always been valuable carpets. The carpet, as well as being an article of high value and a tribute to the deity, is imbued with a mystical atmosphere by its very composition: traditionally, each knot represents a thought conceived by the craftsman while making it.

The ancient Hebrews recognised in this the presence of the Divine Spirit. And there is a significant inscription on an ancient Persian carpet, now in the Poldi Pezzoli Museum, Milan, which reads: 'With the thread of the soul they have woven their warp.'

To try to trace, even approximately, the origins of the Oriental carpet, we must go back to the earliest appearance of the loom, in about 3000 BC, when it was already known and widely used in Egypt. The paintings of Beni Hassan show an abundance of clothing and ornaments, as well as woven materials hanging on the walls or spread on the ground. This is the earliest evidence that has come down to us of textiles on the ground, which the Persians were later to call *ghalli,* meaning something which is trodden upon. But in the East the action of treading on a carpet means living, meditating and praying in close contact with a particular textile, whose outer beauty of design and colour has an intrinsic meaning, embodying the highest ethnic values of these people.

Some centuries later, we find evidence of textiles laid on the ground by the Assyro-Babylonians, highly skilled in the arts of weaving and embroidery, and these can be seen in bas-reliefs of the period in the Louvre and the British Museum. There is no positive evidence of floor-textiles during the Etruscan, Greek and Roman civilisations, but they are mentioned and praised by their historians and poets.

Really genuine knotting—almost exactly as it is

done today—originated in Turkestan. It was there, some two thousand years ago, that the floor-textile became a 'carpet', and there, too, that this particular kind of work took shape and spread throughout the East. It was always by means of a loom that the knots were looped on the warp threads: they were pulled firmly and closely drawn up on the reverse side, then cut at a certain length on the right side, so as to form a soft and warm surface. The number of knots to the square inch varies considerably; in some woollen carpets there are as many as 300, while a silk carpet could have as many as 2000 to the square inch. Only a few primitive tools were used: a rough loom, a shuttle made of metal or wood, a pair of shears, a bodkin, and that was all.

The Turkomans, a people who were for the most part wandering shepherds, were the first to feel the need to make their carpets more hard-wearing. For many decades these were to be all they had in the way of flooring, walls, door, bed, chair, baggage and all that can be used as furniture by people who live in tents, and whose daily life obliges them to be continually on the move. To be on the move means to dismantle and to move one's chattels as easily as possible, and for that kind of life what chattels could be more useful than carpets? During the long trek from one halting-place to the next, the nomad spent his time spinning the wool which would be used for carpet-making. During halts the main occupation was dyeing, a delicate task undertaken by the men; meanwhile the women were entrusted with the actual weaving of the carpet, a craft they learnt at a very early age. Orient means 'light and colour', and no people have a more inborn feeling and love for colour than those of the East. As is written in the ancient scriptures, 'They understand the splendour of the grass and the glory of the flowers'. After years of using wools in their natural colours, that is to say white and brown in all the shades which nature gives to the fleeces of goats, sheep and camels, the earliest sources of the wool used for carpets, the Orientals decided that colour would give their carpets the splendour and beauty of fabrics and ceramics. Unfortunately, with the passage of time most of the ancient formulae have been lost, but we still know the basic sources: thus all shades of blue from ultramarine to pale cobalt come from indigo; red comes from cochineal and cherries, and also from madder, a common enough plant throughout the East, whose roots yield many shades of brick-red, varying according to the district where it is found; yellow comes from various shrubs and berries, and specially from turmeric and saffron; henna, so widely used in the East for dyeing beards and hair, yielded a dark orange-red, while brown came from the gall-nut and from walnut-shells. So much for the basic colours. The different shades were obtained by mixing them —yellow with blue, blue with red, and so on.

When the Mongol invasions led to trade exchanges with China, a secret method of colouring silk, afterwards lost for years, became known. Instead of dyeing the yarn, the Chinese mixed certain vegetable substances into the silkworm's food, so that the thread was no longer produced in the natural colour of silk, but according to the colouring-matter which had been added. Very few colours were produced by this method, but those few sufficed to create veritable masterpieces of technique. The most important factor influencing the whole range of colours, however, is water, and this is affected by temperature, hardness and atmospheric conditions. Exposure to the sun during short or long spells, and the number of rinsings given to the wool have a decisive effect on colour-shades; and often the most unexpected and delightful colour-schemes were, in fact, never intended but brought about by chance and tricks of nature.

The art of dyeing is full of secrets, in some families jealously handed down from father to son as an exclusive heritage not to be divulged to outsiders. Some tribes secretly cultivated plants solely for the purpose of wool-dyeing. These time-honoured processes sometimes produced unexpected results, which is why streaks of a different colour sometimes appear on a carpet just where the pattern calls for the same shade; these are the so-called *abrasc* which are not, as might be expected, counted as faults. On the contrary, it seems that these, with their variations of colour, bring the added charm of the unexpected, especially on carpets with a plain background, where they break the monotony of the monochrome by producing a luminous effect which enlivens the surface of the wool.

The Turkomans, with their endless wanderings, spread the system of carpet-knotting throughout the East. But it was Persia that was to reach the highest peaks of this special art, so that even today Oriental carpets, wherever they come from, are commonly known as 'Persian'.

Some five hundred years before Christ, with the conquest of Babylon, Cyrus the Great opened up new horizons for the Persians. They took over the sumptuous and elaborate designs of Assyro-Babylonian fabrics, usually celebrating important events and immortalising kings and gods in embroidery, and so made carpet-weaving a special and most delicate art of its own. It was an art which expressed the culture and philosophy of this long-suffering and deeply religious people.

With the fall of the Roman Empire and the transfer of the capital to Byzantium, the export of Oriental carpets to the West came to an end. Later on the Crusades were to bring about renewed understanding and appreciation of carpets and their full artistic value.

During centuries of Oriental history, the carpet always emerges victorious from war and devastation. For the conquerors, it is coveted war-booty; for the defeated, there is an age-old tradition to keep alive; and in peace talks it is the propitiatory gift which smoothes the way to a successful agreement. This has always been the way in every age: in the Mahomedan era, six centuries after Christ; during the conquest of Persia by the Arabs, who made their capital in

Damascus; during the different Caliphates, which followed each other for five centuries; down to the invasion in the 13th century of the Mongols, who brought death and destruction everywhere and settled partly in the east of the Caspian Sea (where they are called Turks) and partly in the surrounding districts (where they are called Tartars). Contrary to what might have been expected, these invasions brought new contacts and the carpet became more varied in character. The Ottoman Turks, on their way from central to western Asia, spread the new taste throughout Europe; they also picked up Greek culture, and spread that too, enriched by the Oriental tradition.

With Marco Polo (1254–1324) a new age begins. Artists and craftsmen in different countries are now in touch with each other; of all the arts, that of carpet-making benefits most, being an indispensable part of daily life for most Orientals, who delight in continually inventing new designs and ideas.

Though few technical variations exist between countries in knotting methods and in the materials used for carpet-making, there are infinite differences of pattern and decoration. Those who understand carpets can easily read in them the different traditions, mentality and religion of the various countries. Each main group of carpet-makers, in spite of exchanging patterns and ideas, remains faithful to its own heritage. Even if Iranian work of this period has strange, fabulous animals and patterns, which are Chinese in origin, even if Asia Minor adopts and assimilates certain geometrical designs from the Caucasus, the individual character of the work remains unmistakable. Another instance of interchange between different peoples, which enriched rather than lessened the individuality of the work, occurred a century later, between France and the East. This was in the 18th century, when Oriental craftsmen were invited to France to make Savonnerie carpets. On their return to their own countries they brought with them some French designs, and though orientalised these can be recognised in carpets such as those from Bijar, Senneh, Karabagh and Ghiordes.

The years roll on, history unfolds, but in the East the carpet remains a steadfast star. Not even the massacres and devastations of Tamberlaine, who reigned from 1369 to 1405 and conquered the whole of Asia, could halt the development and continued life of the arts. In Egypt, too, there is increased carpet-making during the Mameluke rule (1250–1517); and all this creative fervour in the Middle East leads in the end to the finest hour of this kind of work, in the reign of Abbas the Great, Shah of Persia, from 1588 to 1629. Innumerable accounts of this time have come down to us from Venetian ambassadors, and particularly from one G. Barbaro, who left inimitable descriptions of the magnificence of the stately homes of Persia and of the royal palace, which at that time was at Tabriz.

At this same time, while in Persia and Asia Minor there is renewed enthusiasm which carries carpet-making to its highest peaks, in Turkestan, on the other hand, it begins to go downhill.

This is because in Turkestan, where the Oriental carpet took shape and developed its characteristic features, it remains fixed in a static pattern, with few individual motifs and no play of fantasy in the colours, perhaps due to the great poverty of the population and to their austere temperament.

The reign of the Shah Abbas the Great, who can be compared with Renaissance rulers for his fostering and patronage of the arts, sees the advent of carpets interwoven with gold, silver and silk, and set with pearls and precious stones. This sumptuous age is described by Sir Anthony Shirley, who visited Persia in 1599 and returned loaded with gifts: 'Forty horses in fine harness, four of them with plated gold saddles stuck with jewels, and two with silver ones. Fifteen camels and another fifteen baggage-mules. Three very fine tents, eighteen carpets, unusually elaborately worked in gold . . .' It was on Shirley's advice that Shah Abbas the Great sent the first embassy from Persia to the courts of Europe.

This was known as the 'mission of the lost carpets' since, according to a contemporary report, the 32 huge coffers containing the gifts, consisting mostly of valuable carpets, were stolen in the city of Archangel. This first mission was followed by many others, and did much to further trade between Europe and the East. Shah Abbas sent a second mission to Venice, where it was welcomed by the Doge Marino Grimani; the carpets brought as gifts on this occasion can still be seen in the Treasury of S. Marco and bear witness to the splendours of the past. Other embassies were answered by missions sent to Persia by many Western monarchs. Never had such a wealth of carpets been seen, all created specially to dazzle the eyes of potentates who vied with each other in opulence and refinement.

In the following century the Afghans rebelled against Persian domination and made their way to the district of Kirman, getting as far as Ispahan, where they were enchanted by art treasures such as they had never before seen. Peter the Great of Russia chose this moment of Persia's weakness to take possession of the provinces around the Caspian Sea, while the Turks occupied the districts of Tabriz, Hamadan and Kirman. Persia, badly governed by the successors of Shah Abbas the Great, was split up and divided between these three groups, who went on squabbling among themselves for power and dynastic rights. The art of carpet-making, however, remained alive under the different rulers; but from this moment it began to go downhill, and never again reached its past splendour.

When Aga Mahomed Khan, of the Kajar dynasty (1796–1925) moved the capital to Teheran, he neglected all the arts except jewellery, to which he devoted himself passionately, spending huge sums on it. Under his successors, Persia went on declining, and all the other carpet-making countries followed suit. For commercial reasons this art, so Eastern in both form and spirit, began to lose its character during the 19th century. European importers, mainly German and English, industrialised it, so that what had hitherto been the genuine expression of the habits, customs and thought of Islam became a large-scale industry aimed at Western customers.

In the last years of the 19th century synthetic dyes and the mechanisation of wool-spinning make their appearance. The wise insistence of the old carpet-makers on using only wool from living animals now began to be neglected, and for this reason we find recent examples of carpets made with lustreless wool which does not wear well and is vulnerable to moths. Designs and shapes were on lines intended to suit European taste, and the Eastern carpet lost its special characteristics. So, if we wish to understand it and consider it in its essential nature, we must study it from its first manifestations down to the beginning of the 19th century, that is to say as long as the carpet retains the character and meaning for which it was created; and we must make use of the evidence to be found in ancient mural paintings and bas-reliefs rather than fragments of carpet which can be seen in the museums.

With this in view, we must not overlook the enormous amount of evidence to be found in the great European painters, from Giotto down to the end of the 19th century—that is to say, as long as painting still has a documentary and decorative content as well as its other intrinsic qualities. Oriental carpets have always held a great attraction for painters: in religious pictures they represent the exaltation of the deity, in portraits of eminent people they add a note of opulence and dignity, and they have an important effect on colour and composition.

In Germany the painter who most often portrayed the Oriental carpet was Hans Holbein in the 16th century. He repeatedly includes in his paintings a type of Ushak (Asia Minor) carpet, to such an extent that even today these are commonly known as Holbein carpets. But the most frequent and inspiring representations of Oriental carpets are to be found in the works of the Italian painters, and these can be briefly listed. From 1200 to 1300 there are Giotto, the Lorenzetti brothers, Simone Martini, and Lippo Memmi. From 1300 to 1500 there are Fra Angelico, Antonello da Messina, Giovanni Bellini, Botticelli, Vittore Carpaccio, Francesco and Jacopo da Ponte, Bassano, Gaudenzio Ferrari, Ghirlandaio, Filippo Lippi, Mantegna, Lorenzo Lotto, Piero della Francesca, Pinturicchio, Pollaiuolo and Titian. From 1500 to 1700 Bronzino, Caravaggio, Giovanni Battista Crespi (known as il Cerano), Sofonisba Anguisciola, Giuseppe Maria Crespi, Daniele da Volterra and the Bascheni. In the 18th century Pietro Longhi is the main exponent, followed in the 19th century by Tranquillo Cremona, Girolamo Induno, Domenico Morelli, Mosè Bianchi and Cesare Tallone, not to mention all the minor and Mannerist painters who portrayed the Oriental carpet for its atmosphere and colour effects. It could also be said that contemporary painters who practise abstract art are not far from some of the patterns of central Asian carpets.

This is enough to place the Oriental carpet among *objets d'art*. If we want to understand the spirit in which these people made their carpets, for the delight of all, knot by knot, and with infinite patience; if we want to understand the thought and philosophy which inspired them, which for us is still something of a closed book, then we must learn to approach them lovingly. This can be done by living in their company, studying them with feeling and handling them as we might a poem or a picture, until this particular form of Oriental art becomes a pleasure and inspiration.

CLASSIFICATION OF CARPETS
KILIMS

Before going on to the classification of carpets, we must pause briefly to consider the Kilim, one of the earliest Oriental fabrics and the ancestor of the typical carpet. This is worked like a tapestry, but by a method which creates two equal surfaces, on the right and reverse sides of the fabric. Where the colours change, thin slits are formed, and these make the carpet as soft and easy to handle as cloth. Today, Kilims are becoming scarce, but at one time they were made in almost all Eastern countries and preserve the character of each country in their designs. Senneh carpets are more delicate, and incredibly fine; Caucasian carpets are even more pleasing, because they make use of the open spaces between the different colours to stress and outline more clearly their characteristic geometric pattern. They were in everyday use by both nomads and settled peoples, and they served as tents, coverings and tablecloths. Their origin goes back to the earliest times.

PERSIA

Persia is seven times the size of Great Britain and occupies a large part of the Iranian tableland, between the Caspian Sea, the Persian Gulf, the Tigris, the Hilmend, Afghanistan and Baluchistan. Iran means 'light', and this agrees with the fact that Persia in the past was always mistress of all the arts. Firdusi (10th century), in his *Book of Kings*, praises the splendour of the ancient Persian Empire, which extended as far as Egypt and the Mediterranean.

Anatolian and Turkoman carpets, the earliest examples of this new art for the Persians, were completely assimilated and modified to fit in with the Persian style, whose naturalistic splendour of decoration was inspired by the finest miniatures and by beautiful bindings of the Koran. The main feature, which totally changes the character of the carpet, is the central medallion, sometimes lobed, sometimes hung with festoons, decorated with pendants, lanterns and rectangular inscriptions. The central motif of the medallion is then repeated at the four corners, the borders are widened and become a splendid frame for the centrepiece, and the design is enriched and filled out. During the Safavid dynasty (1502–1736) the golden age of the Persian carpet, the rule forbidding the representation of living creatures was lifted, and this gave rise to two types which belong exclusively to the Persian tradition: the garden carpet, and the hunting-scene carpet.

The oldest known hunting-scene carpet in Europe is that in the Poldi Pezzoli Museum, Milan. This bears the Mahomedan date 929, which corresponds to our year 1523. (Mahomedan dates can be calculated as follows: from the number 929, subtract 3%, that is to say, 28; to the resulting figure—901—add 622, which is the date of the Hegira, Mahomed's flight from Mecca to Medina, and the answer is 1523.) This carpet in Milan, once belonging to the House of Savoy, is the work of Ghiyas el Din Jami, the most famous Persian carpet-maker of all time and most probably responsible for brocades and velvets worthy of the *Thousand and One Nights*. The Milan hunting-scene carpet is designed so that the scenes can be viewed from all four corners of the carpet, and is full of interesting details such as wild beasts on the prowl, horsemen in the act of hunting and killing them, and animals and birds in a maze of flowers. In the elaborate central medallion an inscription stands out, giving the date and the words written for this work of art by its creator: 'By the labours of Ghiyas el Din Jami this work was brought to its splendid conclusion in the year 929.'

Other equally famous hunting-scene carpets are the Ardebil carpet, dated 1539 (our calendar) and now in the Victoria and Albert Museum, London; the one which formerly belonged to the Austrian court and is now in the Vienna State Museum, with strange winged creatures reproduced from ancient fabrics on its borders; the carpet of the Paris Rothschilds; that of the Duke of Buccleuch; and the one in the Textile Museum at Lyon. And we must not forget the carpets which gleam with gold and silver in the Bardini Museum, Florence, and the Musée des Arts Décoratifs, Paris.

The garden carpet faithfully reproduces garden plants; it is like a gaily filled flowerbed, where animals leap and play and many-coloured birds flutter and swoop, where rippling streams reflect the blue of the sky and gleam with darting fish. Sometimes the garden carpet has a central tree of life, a subject which bodes well for the person for whom the carpet is intended. The tree fills the whole centre of the carpet from top to bottom, spreading its blossoming boughs, among which all kinds of birds hover and settle. It is a delicate symbol of life on earth and hereafter, since a garden has always been thought of as an important source of happiness. The Bible tells of the Garden of Eden, where all kinds of vegetation flourished beneath the tree of life, the tree of the knowledge of good and evil, which was continuously watered by a clear stream. The Koran in its turn promises for the hereafter a life to come which will be passed in two leafy gardens.

An enormous number of flowers is shown in Persian carpets, and most of them grow in Europe—zinnias, asters, chrysanthemums, convolvulus, purslane, tulips, iris and lilies. Narcissi and roses are the favourites: Persians are so fond of roses that on one carpet, in the Victoria and Albert Museum, part of the famous *Ode to the Rose*, by the poet Hafiz, is copied out. Garden carpets show a great variety of leaves; the tree most often seen in them is the cypress, which is sometimes made to appear like a small elongated pyramid. Fruits, too, are often represented, the commonest being the pomegranate, because it symbolises life and prosperity.

Another particularly Persian type is the inscribed carpet. Verses from the Koran, poems and loving messages form highly decorative patterns. One of the most delicately executed inscriptions runs: 'Lift up your head and look at the trees, which at the sunset hour send forth their prayer to the Lord of creation.'

It will be seen that the designers of Persian carpets belonged to the cultivated class and were true artists. The gracefulness of the intricate patterns reflects the Persian mind—versatile, subtle, thoughtful and at the same time imaginative. An old motto says of the Persian, 'He tries to unravel a knot of the universal skein, and entangles it even more.' Talent, aspiration and achievement in an endless round.

To make a list of names of Persian carpets would be a long and arduous task, because too many names belong to the same districts and so produce the same type of work. It will be sufficient to point out that normally the double knot, known as 'Senneh', is used, while the single 'Ghiordes' knot is rarely found; that the warp and the weft are generally in flax or cotton and the surfaces in wool, except for a few valuable examples which either have the weft in silk or else are entirely worked in silk. Here, then, is a summary of the main types of Persian carpet.

Bakhtiari. Bakhtiari carpets are made by nomad tribes who wander through the valleys and mountains of the district to the north of Shiraz, in the province of

Fars. They have bright colours and their designs break up the background into differently coloured sections. The whole carpet is entirely covered in floral decoration, the borders being in several bands around a wide central strip. They are very well made and pleasing to the eye because of their bright and varied colouring.

Bijar. In and around Bijar, to the north of Senneh, they make a type of carpet exceptional for the compact closeness of its knotting. They are hard-wearing, heavy carpets, with clear-cut patterns, which show the whole range of Persian designs; large blue medallions stand out against a background of dark pink, and the borders repeat the pattern of the medallions. Others have small, crowded designs, almost like Senneh carpets, while of course many are openly based on European styles, reproducing flowers, especially roses, like those of French carpets.

Feraghan and Mahal. The Feraghan plateau is surrounded by mountains and lies halfway between Teheran and Ispahan. It is a region of scattered villages, all busily engaged in carpet-making, and is rich in pastureland and luxuriant vegetation useful for wool-dyeing purposes. It is this vegetation which inspires the close-packed designs of small many-coloured flowers. Sometimes we find flowers, usually yellow, in the form of small trees, in rows, scattered here and there on the background of the carpet. There is also a central medallion, or else rhomboids, but these are invariably connected with the floral designs. The borders are important, linear, and crowded with little flowers. Modern examples, too, although far removed from the quality of the old carpets, are good, well made, and varied in form.

In the Feraghan district there are also several centres where they make a type of carpet known as 'Mahal'; the name means 'village' and does not refer to a particular locality. These are rather coarse carpets, but they are very like Feraghan work in their sturdiness and their warm colouring.

Qum and Naim. These are very recent types, and represent the best modern Persian work. Closely knotted, they reproduce the best-known patterns of the old Persian carpets, usually against a light background. They do not belong exclusively to any one tradition, as this district, to the south of Teheran, has been developed only recently, when oil was discovered there. Industrialisation has made it one of the most important markets for Persian carpets.

Hamadan. Hamadan is an ancient city, whose main population is Jewish. The town and surrounding district have a large output of carpets, and a busy market for them. The old carpets are considered real masterpieces, in contrast to coarse and inferior modern work. However, they all have clearly recognisable characteristics, with dark geometrical medallions standing out against a background of natural camelhair. They vary a great deal in size, and runners and saddlebags are quite common.

Heriz, Gorevan, Serab and Bagshaish. In the Heriz district, which lies in the mountain country of Azerbaijan, to the east of Tabriz and south-west of the Caspian Sea, they make carpets which have different names but are really the same, in design, workmanship and the quality of the wool. The oldest types are the Heriz carpets, which were succeeded by Gorevan, Serab and Bagshaish carpets. Somewhat large and rectangular, they are made with sizeable knots and have stylised, geometrical floral patterns with a very clear background. The colours are bright.

Herat. Herat is an ancient Persian city, situated between Khorassan and Afghanistan on the road to Bokhara and Kashmir. In the time of Shah Abbas the Great it was among the most important cultural centres of Persia and one of the most famous of carpet markets. Very fine wool and silk are produced in the district. A typical motif is the closed rosette in elongated leaves, or else the ribbon-pattern scroll, which originated in China. Another common motif is the diamond, standing above the rosette with its eight points. Often, too, we find the palm-leaf, in an elongated form as in the Indian tradition. The background is dark blue or purple-red and the main colour of the border a fine green, setting off the yellow and ivory pattern elegantly and harmoniously. The knotting is thick and accurate and the wool very rich. Sometimes silk is used, too, though only in the weft, and this makes the carpets unusually splendid. They are rectangular—twice as long as they are broad—and esteemed valuable traditional carpets.

Ispahan. Ispahan carpets are generally old and belong to the time of Shah Abbas the Great, when Ispahan was the capital of Persia. They take their place among the artistic treasures of Persia and are known as 'the Shahs' carpets'. Very finely worked, often in silk, gold and silver, they have a broad background of a magnificent wine-red colour: on this an elegant and restful arabesque unfolds, with the palm-leaf dominating other elongated leaves. The border is broad, enclosed between two smaller bands whose background of old gold and green sets off large floral patterns. The output of genuine Ispahan carpets may be said to have ended in the early 18th century, when the Afghan hordes reduced this fine city, known as 'the pearl of Persia', to a heap of ruins. Later they started making carpets again, but these cannot compare with the early ones.

Karaja. Karaja is a northern province, bordered and influenced by the Caucasus and Armenia. Its carpets are made wholly of wool, and their decoration ranges from the floral to the geometrical. Contemporary workers also produce good carpets, always very long and extremely elegant. The beauty of their colours is partly due to a special quality of the water in which the wool is washed, giving the carpets softness and an unusual colour-range.

Kashan. From earliest times Kashan, lying on the Iran tableland between Teheran and Ispahan, was a very important artistic centre. But the remarkable thing is that the high standard of its output, far from being the result of a happy life and a favourable geographical position, was in fact the outcome of adversity. The population, which lives in hovels built on the ancient ruins, is continually harassed by scorpions and other dangerous creatures, and by a hot tropical climate. Even today these unfortunate people weave carpets worthy of their glorious past: in the history of Persian carpet-making no other centre has ever excelled Kashan, where the finest woollen and silk carpets are made. They are finely knotted and their wool is unusually soft and silky. The patterns portray flowers and animals which sometimes look as if they have been drawn with a pen. Such harmony of colouring is rarely to be seen elsewhere. The 'holy carpet of the Mosque of Ardebil', known throughout the world and now in the Victoria and Albert Museum, was made in Kashan. It is an example of 16th-century work, with pale yellow festoons on its central medallion, standing out against a blue background covered in floral garlands and with figures which look as if they have been chiselled; lanterns hang from the medallion. In the borders, too, are human figures in various attitudes, surrounded by a profusion of flowering shrubs. On a rectangular panel, inserted on one side of the smaller border, are the words: 'I have no other refuge in the world than thy threshold, my head has no other shelter than thy doorway. The slave Maksun of Kashan toiled in this blessed handiwork, 946'—which corresponds to our year 1539.

One such example suffices to establish the eternal

renown of the carpets made in Kashan. Even today work done there is among the best in all Persia.

Kirman. The Kirman district is in south-eastern Persia, far off the beaten track and consequently work there has always kept distinct characteristics, uninfluenced by foreign tastes and styles. The population consists of nomads and settled groups, all Iranian by race. They breed sheep which yield an extremely soft and silky wool, as well as camels producing hair which is very like Kashmir camelhair. Moreover, the local water is chemically well suited to wool-dyeing. The knotters are true artists, and their skill is so consummate that Kirman carpets have been called 'jewels of the loom'. Their main decoration consists of birds and all kinds of flowers, arranged with a rich freedom of imagination on lightly and delicately coloured backgrounds. The borders, rich and thick with flowers, form a superb frame to the main design, whose predominant flower is the rose. In the 18th century, Kirman knotters were in almost universal demand for their mastery of this incomparable art. It was at Rawar, of all the Kirman villages, that knotting had reached its greatest heights when, in the 19th century, a group of German traders industrialised the production of Kirman carpets there; not being able to pronounce the name correctly, the Germans said 'Laver', and even today the name 'Laver' is a byword for quality in a Kirman carpet. It is said that their decoration is Indian in origin. Kirman has in fact had an enormous influence on all Persian carpet-making.

1. Ancient Ushak carpet, known as the 'Holbein'. 16th century (Asia Minor). Bardini Museum, Florence.

2. Ladik prayer-rug. 17th century (Asia Minor). Bardini ·
Museum, Florence.

3. Ancient Persian hunting-scene carpet (detail). 16th century. Poldi Pezzoli Museum, Milan.

4. Ancient Persian carpet with inscriptions. 16th century.
Poldi Pezzoli Museum, Milan.

5. Ancient Tabriz carpet (detail). First half of 16th century
(Persia). Musée des Arts Décoratifs, Paris.

6. Ancient Tabriz carpet (detail). First half of 16th century
(Persia). Musée des Arts Décoratifs, Paris.

7. Ardebil carpet with inscriptions. Dated 946 (AD 1539).
Victoria and Albert Museum, London.

8. Ancient hunting-scene carpet (detail). 16th century (northern Persia). Musée des Arts Décoratifs, Paris.

9. Fragment of an ancient Persian carpet, called 'Polish', Kunstgewerbemuseum, Vienna.

10. Carpet with medallions (detail). 16th century (Persia).
Victoria and Albert Museum, London.

11. Ancient Persian carpet, called 'Polish'. 17th centur
Kunstgewerbemuseum, Vienn

12. Bakhtiari carpet. 19th century (Persia). Private collection, Milan.

13. Bijar carpet. 19th century (Persia). Private collection, Milan.

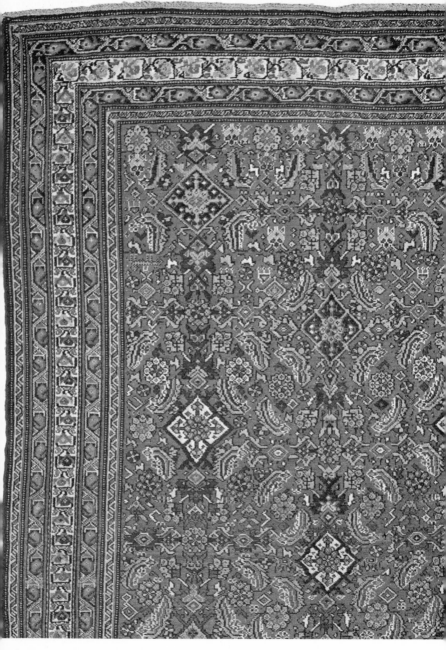

14. Feraghan carpet. 19th century (Persia). Private collection, Milan.

15. Naim carpet. 20th century (Persia). Private collection, Milan.

16. Hamadan carpet (detail). 19th century (Persia). Private collection, Milan.

Khorassan and Meshed. The northernmost province of Persia is Khorassan, known as 'the land of the sun', and Meshed is its capital. Hemmed in by a mountain chain and a desert, its geographical position subjects it to a very varied climate; and varied, too, is its heterogeneous population, consisting of Arabs, Turkomans, Turks, Armenians, Jews (mainly nomadic) and a few Iranians. Unexpectedly, this ethnic mixture has contributed greatly to the cultural and artistic life of the people, who are exceptionally versatile.

Khorassan carpets have all the characteristics of Meshed specimens, differing mainly in their more accurate workmanship and the soft and silky quality of the wool. They have a deep, soft pile, usually with close-packed floral designs, and sometimes animal figures, standing out from a blue or red background. The borders, always rich and splendid, have the palmette and rosette with other small floral patterns featured in the central strip; these make an imposing frame for the main composition, which usually includes the rosette at the centre of a medallion. At the corners we find another motif which is a favourite in this district—the palm-leaf. The whole effect is one of elegance, the lustre of the wool making it even more attractive.

Kurdistan. In the extreme north-west of Persia lies the district of Kurdistan, where they make carpets which have no specially clear-cut characteristics; having no tradition to follow, they imitate Persian,

Turkish and Caucasian designs in turn. However, the work is pleasant and of excellent quality.

Saruk. Saruk is a little village in the mountainous part of Feraghan and produces characteristic carpets uninfluenced by work from other districts. The design, the colours and the style are manifestly Persian. Against a background which is generally red or blue, floral motifs are picked out with great realism, enriching the sumptuous medallions with their irregular outlines. The border is composed of a wide, broadly designed band, framed by other smaller bands. The colours, dark in tone, are rich and warm with here and there a bright touch. The workmanship is very tight and close-packed and its fineness can compare with the best Kirman and Senneh carpets. Unlike them, however, Saruk carpets are robust and hard-wearing, another effect of the extraordinary quality of the wool.

Shiraz, Afshar and Kashkai. Shiraz, the present capital of the province of Fars, is a city near ancient Persepolis, famed in the old days for its poets, its treasures and its gardens, where equally famous nightingales used to sing. In addition to this, and to explain the fascination the district has for the tourist, we must not forget that this lovely valley surrounded by mountains is where Cyrus the Great is buried and Alexander enjoyed spending long visits; it was a favourite haunt of Shah Abbas the Great and its praises were sung by the great Persian poets Sadi and

Hafiz. For Christians, it is one of the halting-places in the long journey of the Magi. The population is proud to belong to the purest Aryan stock, which originally came from the Caucasus.

Shiraz carpets are made entirely of wool and are very soft and glossy; the workmanship is rather loose and so the carpets are less hard-wearing. Carpets made in the same district at Afshar and Kashkai are of this same type. They show Caucasian influence, introduced by nomads from the Caucasus, who settled in Shiraz and brought with them the taste for geometrical patterns. Rhomboid medallions are arranged in a row in the centre of the composition and are surrounded by small stylised flower and animal motifs in dark colours, which tend to become monotonous. It can be said that this group is somewhat inferior to other Persian carpets.

Shiraz workmanship is better than that of Afshar and Kashkai, perhaps as a result of the reign of Karim Khan (1760–1779) when the capital of Persia was moved to Shiraz. At that time the city excelled in all the arts and had a fine carpet-works, of which it was justifiably proud. Sometimes the name of Mecca is found alongside that of Shiraz. This applies to carpets which pilgrims took with them to Mecca for their own personal use or as offerings at the temple, or perhaps as merchandise to barter and sell. Hence their poor and flabby workmanship, since the carpets had to be very light and easy to handle.

Senneh. In the neighbourhood of Senneh, which lies

near the borders of Kurdistan, in north-west Persia, are found some of the finest Persian carpets. In spite of European influence on the adjoining countries, the Senneh district has managed to preserve its own individual character. The workmanship is very fine and small, double-knotted, and of the kind in general use almost throughout Persia. The wool is really exceptional in quality since it is invariably and exclusively taken from young animals. The tiny pattern spreads closely over the whole composition and there is sometimes a lozenge at the centre. The colours are sober and the borders narrow and simple. The motif which crops up repeatedly is the palmette, and this is sometimes distorted, which is why it is commonly described as 'the fish'. On the whole the carpets give the impression of a mosaic and are so fine to the touch that they seem more like velvets or fabrics than carpets. The knot is made with such incredible skill that it is sometimes hard to believe that these carpets are hand-made.

Serabend Mir. To the south of Feraghan, in several villages scattered on the hillsides, is the home of the carpets called Serabend, with sometimes the name of Mir, an ancient city which was destroyed in an earthquake, suffixed to the name. These have some of the characteristics of Feraghan carpets and invariably include the Indian palmette design, though in a slightly modified form which has led to its being described as a 'pear'. This motif is repeated in continuous rows, with the palmette points facing alternately right and left. The pattern has been used since ancient times in this hilly district, which is so traditionalist that it has always refused to accept outside designs. Sooner than follow foreign influences—which inexorably creep in to some extent everywhere, with the more widespread practice of the art of knotting—these people have gradually given up carpet-making. Consequently Serabend Mir carpets have become rare and hard to come by. They are accurately made, with colours which are calm and restful and at the same time rich and warm. In spite of their lack of variety, they are never monotonous; in fact they have a special distinction and elegance of their own.

Sultanabad. The Sultanabad district, which lies to the north-west of Ispahan, is very picturesque, with mountains and fertile plains rich in flowers. The carpets are made both by inhabitants of the scattered local villages and by nomads, who live on the hills during the hot summers and come down to the valleys in the winter.

Work is now industrialised here, thanks to Europeans who commission work from the local people, supplying them with both materials and designs. In spite of this, the carpets are well made and artistic. They are generally large, and of first-class quality.

Tabriz. In the north-west of Persia stands the city of Tabriz, capital of Azerbaijan. It is surrounded by fertile country, rich in meadows which provide excellent pasture for sheep and camels. Tabriz is an important centre for the making and selling of a wide range of carpets, from carelessly made ones to work which deserves a place in any of the finest collections.

' The favourite plan is that of a central medallion, repeated at the four corners; the main ground is floral and the borders often contain inscriptions inside rectangular panels. In ornamentation, old Tabriz carpets are very similar to those from Kirman and Kashan. They are hard-wearing and long-lasting, and are to be seen in many parts of the world. Red, blue and ivory are the most usual backgrounds, and the patterns are in various pleasant colours. With the passage of time they have lost their specifically Oriental characteristics and there is a great variety of size and shape to meet all tastes and requirements.

Teheran. At Teheran, the present capital of Persia, there is no real carpet-making tradition, so the city cannot claim to be the home of any ancient and famous examples. Good carpets are, however, made there and are of good craftsmanship, though without any distinguishing characteristics.

ASIA MINOR

Asia Minor is rich in mountains and valleys, rising to the Black Sea in the north, and towards the Mediterranean to the west and south. Its population, which is generally thought of as Turkish, is a mixture of pure Greek elements, Kurds, Turkomans, Armenians, Jews and Europeans who, except in some centres which have been influenced by the West, still lead very primitive lives. It is one of the richest parts of the world in ancient history, since it includes the Greek territory where Homer was born, and its marvellous civilisation was assimilated first by the Persians, then by the Romans, and later still by the Turks. Its history is also connected with the story of Jesus Christ, and of the Crusades, which led the way to Palestine. It is the scene of an extraordinary stratification of races, religions and civilisations, and these are faithfully mirrored in the Anatolian carpet which changes its outward form as it reflects changing events.

During the first years of the 11th century, after being conquered by the Arabs and strenuously resisting the Mongol invasion, this rich and fertile country succumbed to the Turkoman hordes, who called it Anatolia, meaning the 'Country of the Rising Sun'. It was from the Turkomans that the Turks learned the art of knotting, but they brought this to such a pitch of perfection that the single Turkish or Ghiordes knot, together with the double Persian or Senneh knot, came to be used throughout the East.

In the 13th century a group of wandering horsemen, led by Ertoghrul, through their love of adventure and a fighting spirit, were fired to join the Turks in their struggle against the invader. After a victory they pitched camp in the region south of Constantinople, the ancient Istanbul. This is the origin of the Turkish Empire, later to be known as the Ottoman empire from the name of Osman, son of Ertoghrul, who succeeded in extending his boundaries beyond the surrounding territories until he had gained possession of all the coastal regions. The Ottoman dynasty was a victorious line, which conquered Nicaea, Kossovo, Nikopolis, Istanbul, Kurdistan, Syria and part of Egypt. Side by side with the growth of the imperial power went that of the arts, including that of carpet-making, whose golden age was in the 15th, 16th and 17th centuries.

The first and most typical carpets of this period are to be found in the pictures of the great painters of the time, above all the Italians, who appreciated to the full their qualities of composition and colour. The favourite carpet of Western painters is the Ushak, which later came to be known as 'the painters' carpet' or, as mentioned earlier, the 'Holbein'.

Anatolian carpets were the most widely known and valued in Europe for their special beauty of design, their brilliant and lovely colours, their small size which made them easy to handle and transport and above all for their 'prayer-rugs', which are quite different from all others.

In the second half of the 15th century, during the reign of Mahomed II (who was known as the Conqueror), the old type of Anatolian carpet was even further enriched by new decorative features which were Persian and Chinese in origin. These belong to the most glorious period of Turkish history, which saw the conquest of Constantinople, a victory which had an element of the miraculous in the cunning and the almost superhuman means employed, as well as in the appearance and use of the earliest fire-arms.

During the reign (1512–1520) of Selim the Fierce, who was led by religious fanaticism to commit unheard of crimes and outrages, the Turks conquered Tabriz, then the capital of Persia. The Sultan summoned to his court artists, poets and philosophers from all parts, and the splendour of this age was matched by the splendour of the Turkish carpets. Prayer-rugs now make their appearance, with their central representation of the *mihrab* (a niche in the *kiblah* wall of a mosque, indicating the direction of Mecca). The niche has a sharply pointed apex, worked in one colour, and at the centre, when this is not completely empty, there hangs a single ornament: a lantern, or a bunch of flowers or some other feature connected with sacred ritual objects. The faithful, wherever they are, at the hour of sunset spread their carpets on the ground, kneel on the *mihrab* and pray, always facing towards Mecca, and with heads bowed on the apex of the niche.

Sometimes the whole of the niche is filled with the tree of life, symbol of the hope for immortality. The borders, decorated with small flowers—roses and carnations are the favourites—are like thin ribbons, one beside the other, usually seven in number, representing the 'seven heavens created by Allah'.

The decorations surrounding the *mihrab* are like a book, in which the devout read their prayers, no matter whether the carpet is destined for Mecca, dedicated to the purpose of reverencing the dead, or forming part of the trousseau of a bride-to-be. The prayer-rug is the inseparable companion of every good Mahomedan, who is never parted from it in peace or war. Most touching of all are the prayer-rugs which call for several prayers, carpets made so that husband and wife, or a whole family, can pray together; these have two, three and up to ten niches and it is affecting to think of all these people united in a single religious impulse and in affectionate family communion. More linear and restful are the carpets known as 'cemetery rugs', which Mahomedans take to the cemetery to pray upon by the tomb of the dear departed. These are not designed predominantly for pleasing effects of colour and decoration; the eye is caught by the stylised image of the funeral pillar and the cypress, repeated several times in succession in or around the niche, and evoke the intimacy of communion with the hereafter. Noblest of all are the prayer-rugs on a white ground, brought as dowries by girls of good families. Each rug expresses personal feelings and a close attachment to tradition, which is proof against the temptations of outside influences and the desire for novelty.

The Mahomedan religion is more orthodox in Turkey than in Persia, and the rule which forbids the representation of living creatures persists longer there. For this reason, Anatolian carpets are almost exclusively floral in their decoration. Green is forbidden as a background colour because Mahomed's banner was green; it must not be trodden upon, and only in fervent prayer may the devout Mahomedan kneel upon it. Therefore green is seldom to be seen, and only in the niche or *mihrab* of certain prayer-rugs, or else only here and there in some unimportant touches of decoration. However, as time went on the custom of not representing living things was relaxed and carpets are seen to include portraits of rulers and other famous people, sometimes even of Europeans.

The conquest of Persia was followed by that of Egypt, and the Turks took over the refinements and culture which had created a highly cultivated society in Cairo. This is the period of Syrian and Damascan carpets, made in Egypt and Syria during the Turkish conquest. With Suleiman the Magnificent (reigned 1520–1566) the Turkish empire extended from Persia as far as Hungary, Vienna, Rhodes and Spain. The carpet-makers in these countries worked on their own, and yet their output is always thought of as Anatolian. Similarly, the Hispano-Moorish carpets made in Istanbul by Persians and commissioned by Turks were likewise called Anatolian.

The reign of Selim II, son of Suleiman the Magnificent, was a period of two new types of carpet, both with white backgrounds; one was known as 'the birds' and the other as 'the cloud and circles'. The first of these features a pattern of S-shaped, stylised leaves, which at first sight seem like a kind of dove and which is repeated throughout the carpet's main pattern. The second kind has a pattern of Chinese origin, consisting of two small wavy strips super-imposed, and surmounted by three small circles placed in a triangle, thus: ⚯ . This forms Tamberlaine's crest and symbolises his dominion over the three divisions of the world.

In spite of the disruptive influence of various countries, Turkish carpets are always elegant and harmonious and manage to preserve their own character intact. In the West they have long been sought after as true works of art.

The beginning of the decadence of this great country is reflected in its 18th-century carpets, which eventually became coarse and nasty, with clashing colours inspired neither by artistic feeling nor by personal affection. Towards the end of the 19th century there seemed to be something of a revival, inspired by European demands, and even today work of this period can be found which has taste and quality. But the recent wars have irrevocably impoverished these people, the land has lost its fertility and the wool-producing flocks have for the most part been sacrificed. Modern carpet-making in Anatolia today has become a handicraft which has lost its intrinsic worth. A few words inscribed in the border of a prayer-rug, now in the Metropolitan Museum, New York, can help us to understand genuine Turkish carpets, which express the character of this heterogeneous and tormented people, sustained as they are by a profound and indestructible faith: 'He [God] knows that which was before and that which shall come after them; they understand nothing of what He knows, only what He wishes . . .'

Caesarea, Panderman and Brussa. Caesarea lies by the

lake of that name, in the eastern part of Anatolia, south-east of Ankara. At present it is the most important market in the whole neighbourhood, and carpet-making there is in the hands of Armenians and Greeks. The carpets are small and are copies of old Turkish prayer-rugs. They are finely knotted, both warp and weft are of cotton, and the surface is either wool or silk. Nevertheless they are second-rate in quality and similar to those made in Brussa, Panderman and around the Sea of Marmara, with which they are often confused.

Damascan or Syrian. These are Anatolian carpets which are called Damascan or Syrian from the places where they are obtained, and because they are shipped to the port of Damascus before being sent to the West. The old carpets, made in the Sultan's workshops at Constantinople, are impossible to come by and seen only in museums and important collections. They are finely worked in Angora wool, with warp and weft in cotton. Some are worked in silk and have a special delicacy of their own, which accentuates the yellow, blue and light green shades which merge with cherry-red, the predominant colour. Generally the main composition is divided into large blocks, each containing an octagon with oblong panels at its sides. The designs which cover the background are minute and represent stylised stars and phials as well as the Chinese cloud, palmettes, leaves and rosettes in the Persian style. The central band of the border is usually filled with oblong blocks containing small patterns and surrounded by arabesques. The carpets look like minute and close-packed mosaics, accurately worked, and are truly masterpieces.

Ghiordes and Bassra Ghiordes. The most famous carpets are made at Ghiordes, a small city to the north-east of Smyrna and the largest and most important carpet-producing centre in Asia Minor. The Ghiordes (or Gordian) knot, which gave its name to the craftsmanship of the majority of Oriental carpets, was made famous in antiquity by Alexander the Great who, when he could not untie it, cut it with a stroke of his sword. Ghiordes carpets are almost all prayer-rugs and the most typical examples of Anatolian work. Their warp and weft are cotton, the surface is worked in wool and they achieve a truly amazing perfection of compositional balance. The niche is sometimes empty and sometimes has the lamp or flowers, or the lateral columns representing the entrance to the temple. It is enclosed above and below by ornamental panels, bearing inscriptions or floral designs, among which the carnation appears most frequently. The borders are numerous and slender, like ribbons one behind the other, and filled with tiny flowers; there is always an odd number of borders—usually seven, like the heavens of Allah. Modern work is very inferior, but until the end of the 19th century Ghiordes carpets were among the finest in the East, both for the range of their colours and for the noble artistic inspiration which pervades them.

Hereke. Hereke carpets are made exclusively in the

Imperial Factory (today the State Factory) in the city of Hereke, situated on the Sea of Marmara. This explains the fine quality of the materials used, whether wool or silk. There are all sizes of Hereke carpets, from very large to very small. While the prayer-rugs clearly reveal their Anatolian origin, the others show a definitely Persian influence, since most of the carpet-makers came from the Kirman district. Those worked in wool have cotton warp and weft, while those worked in silk have warp and weft of silk too.

Kirshir. Kirshir is a village in the heart of Asia Minor, where they make carpets in vivid and brilliant colours, predominantly red and light green. They are worked in rather loose knots, with warp, weft and surfaces in wool; their pile is not very closely shorn and the design is geometrical with large lozenges. They are generally small, or else long and narrow. Modern work may be said to be non-existent, or if it exists it is of the poorest quality.

Kula. Kula is a small centre to the east of Ushak, and in the past it produced magnificent prayer-rugs. They are worked entirely in wool, with a rather loose Ghiordes knot. The main colours are pea-green and blue. Often the niche is divided throughout its length by a bough of blossom, and beside this stylised patterns of trees, funeral columns and small images of mosques are sometimes to be seen; these are the 'cemetery' carpets so dear to Mahomedans. The apex of the niche is always more rounded than in the other carpets. They are masterpieces of simplicity and elegance.

Ladik. The ancient Laodicea, now known as Ladik, is a production centre of very rare prayer-rugs. The niche, almost always wine-red, is topped by a section which contains the elegant motif of 'Rhodes lilies' or tulips. Ladik carpets are always very fine and much sought after by collectors, both for the special elegance of the composition and for the striking greens and yellows which contrast vividly with the red of the niche. The Ghiordes knotting is extremely accurate and results in a firm and exactly proportioned carpet.

Melas. Melas is a city to the south of Smyrna, close to the Aegean Sea. The carpets produced there are in stylised floral patterns and bright colours, with vivid red always predominating. They are made with a rather loose knot and the borders consist of a number of different bands, with a broad spacious one in the middle. Apart from the old carpets, which are jewels of taste and elegance, Melas work is almost always commonplace.

Pergamos. North of Smyrna, opposite the island of Mytilene, is the site of ancient Pergamos, where material for writing on was produced from animals' hides. In antiquity this was used for documents and called *pergamene* (parchment) from its place of origin. Here the carpets are made by nomads or refugees

17. Heriz carpet (detail). 19th century (Persia). Private collection, Milan.

18. Ancient Herat carpet (detail). 17th century (Persia). Bardini Museum, Florence.

19. Karaja carpet (detail). 19th century (Persia). Private collection, Milan.

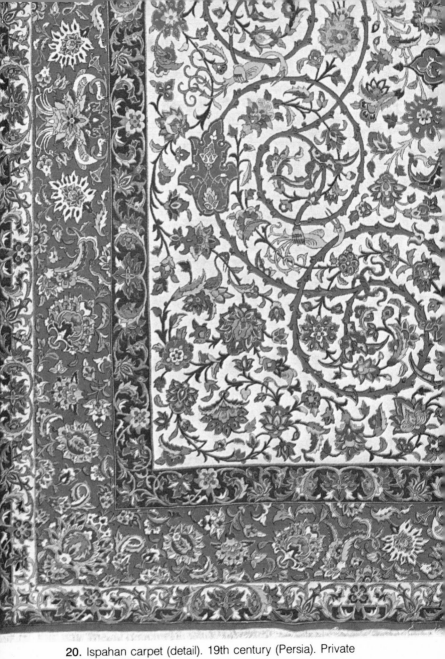

20. Ispahan carpet (detail). 19th century (Persia). Private collection. Milan.

21. Kashan carpet. 19th century (Persia). Private collection, Milan.

23. Khorassan carpet (detail). 19th century (Persia). Private collection, Milan.

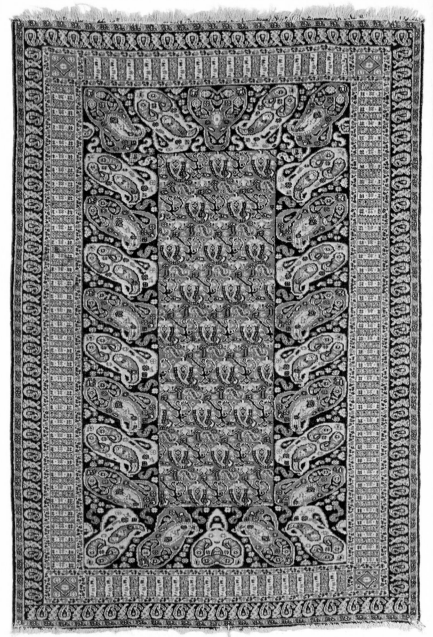

26. Shiraz carpet. 19th century (Persia). Private collection, Milan.

27. Senneh carpet. 19th century (Persia). Private collection, Milan.

28. Serabend Mir carpet (detail). 19th century (Persia).
Private collection, Milan.

29. Teheran carpet. 20th century (Persia).
Private collection, Milan.

30. Tabriz carpet (detail). 19th century (Persia). Private collection, Milan.

31. Prayer-rug from Caesarea or Panderman. 19th century
(Asia Minor). Private collection, Milan.

32. Syrian or Damascan carpet from the court workshop.
16th century. Pogliaghi Collection, Varese.

33. Ghiordes prayer-rug. 18th century (Asia Minor). Private collection, Milan.

34. Bassra Ghiordes carpet. 17th century (Asia Minor). Private collection, Milan.

35. Hereke prayer-rug. 18th century (Asia Minor). Private collection, Milan.

36. Kirshir carpet (detail). 18th century (Asia Minor). Private collection, Milan.

37. Kula prayer-rug. 18th century (Asia Minor). Private collection, Milan.

38. Melas carpet. 18th century (Asia Minor). Private collection, Varese.

39. Pergamos carpet (detail). 18th century (Asia Minor).
Private collection, Milan.

40. Sivas carpet. 19th century (Asia Minor).
Private collection, Milan.

41. Transylvania or Siebenbürgen prayer-rug. 17th-18th
centuries (Asia Minor). Private collection, Monza.

42. Armenian carpet (detail). 18th century (southern Caucasus). Private collection, Monza.

43. Daghestan carpet (detail). 19th century (Caucasus). Private collection, Milan.

44. Derbent carpet (detail). 19th century (Caucasus). Private collection, Milan.

45. Karabagh carpet. 19th century (Caucasus). Private collection, Milan.

46. Seichur carpet. 19th century (Caucasus). Private collection, Milan.

47. Kazak carpet. 19th century (Caucasus). Private collection, Varese.

48. Kazak carpet, with representations of crab, tarantula and diamond. 19th century (Caucasus). Private collection, Milan.

from adjoining countries, and for this reason they have lost their Anatolian character and illustrate, more than anything else, typical Caucasian geometrical designs. They are worked in a rather loose knot, with a thick pile, glossy, brilliant and vividly coloured. Unlike Caucasian carpets, they have both warp and weft in cotton. They are pleasing and attractive carpets and have decorative, original and unusual qualities.

Sivas. Sivas is a city of central Asia which, because of its geographical position, has been continually subjected to invasions. This is why its output of carpets, which were made by settled inhabitants, shows such variations of taste and workmanship. They have warp and weft in cotton and the surfaces are of wool, dyed in delicate and pleasant pastel shades. In general they copy Persian floral models.

Smyrna and Sparta. Smyrna is a large city with important maritime traffic on the Aegean Sea and a vast centre for the buying and selling of carpets. These do not have specially marked characteristics. Designs are sometimes Persian in style, sometimes Turkish, and the workmanship, with warp and weft in cotton and surfaces in wool, is very clumsy. The carpets are aimed exclusively at the export market.

To the east of Smyrna is Sparta, which has nothing to do with the ancient Greek country. Its carpet output resembles that of Smyrna in all respects.

Ushak. A magic word, because, as we have seen, it is the name of the carpets which appear most in the pictures of the great painters of the past. Ushak is a small centre in the interior of Anatolia, to the south of Istanbul, between Ghiordes and Kula. In the past it produced incomparable carpets, which today have altogether disappeared. There is no point in mentioning its modern output because it is so clumsy and inferior.

The old carpets generally have a red or deep blue ground, which displays a symmetrical pattern of large stars, or else a central medallion reaching sideways to the borders and repeated in halves at both ends of the carpet. The whole design is decorated with stylised floral arabesques in yellow, blue, green, ivory or red. The central band of the border is rather broad and has two narrow bands on either side of it. The so-called 'Holbein' carpet is also from Ushak, and has a light red ground, setting off a continuous yellow arabesque design, which is emphasised here and there with touches of dark blue. Ushak carpets are made entirely of wool.

Transylvania or Siebenbürgen. The Transylvanian carpet, almost always a small prayer-rug, is also called Siebenbürgen, because the Turkish armies who besieged Vienna in the 17th century accumulated a huge supply of carpets in the little town of Siebenbürgen (which means 'seven castles'). These ended up by belonging to the local inhabitants and to the churches of Transylvania. They are exclusively ancient carpets, finely knotted, with warp and weft sometimes in wool, sometimes in cotton. Their design is distinctively Anatolian, with occasional evidence of Persian influence; the colours are light and lively and distinguished by contrasts of white and yellow. Some are very similar to Ushak carpets, some feature the Chinese cloud motif; others have Tamberlaine's cloud pattern, with the three circles, a design known in Germany as 'thunder and lightning'; yet others have a stylised bird theme. These carpets are now in museums or private collections, and they, too, belong to the type reproduced in the works of the old masters.

CAUCASUS

The Caucasus is a mountainous region, lying between the Black Sea and the Caspian and bordering on Persia to the south and Turkey to the south-west. The chain of mountains which crosses it from north-west to south-east is like an insurmountable barrier with one single gap, the Dariel Pass, dominated by Queen Tamara's castle. The Caucasus can never become an independent state because it is continually subject to invasions and is aimed at as a refuge by expatriates. We can go back in history to the time when the Caucasus was a Persian colony, until in 323 BC it became the northern frontier of Alexander the Great's Asiatic territories. Two centuries later, Armenia annexed the southern part and Persia and other neighbouring countries took the rest. Crushed and abandoned at the same time, the Caucasus became both the home and the prey of a variety of populations. Its golden age was the 12th century, when the reign of Queen Tamara shone like a single star; it was a century of resistance against its enemies, and the only period when the Caucasus was really and truly an independent state. But the hordes of Genghis Khan drove the local inhabitants into the mountains, where they settled in the narrow and almost impassable valleys and divided into different groups. Hence the variety of Caucasian carpets, each belonging to a separate group, with its own completely individual characteristics. The only thing they have in common is their square and positive design, which reflects their bleak landscape.

During the reign of Peter the Great of Russia (1689–1725), Persia was compelled to yield the eastern part of the Caucasus and part of the Armenian tableland to Russia. Turkey, too, had to give up the territory it had conquered in its day, and Russia set to work to subjugate the Caucasian peoples—an operation which cost them thirty years of strife, because they came up against a determined resistance, directed and led by Shamyl, the national hero of the Caucasus. Sooner than surrender, the Circassian tribe emigrated *en masse* to Anatolia, and from there dispersed to Constantinople. Thus the population of the Caucasus is even more mixed than in ancient times; but this has not destroyed tradition, since each group keeps to itself and even today speaks its own language and follows its own customs and habits with obstinate and steadfast fidelity. The tribes are for the most part occupied with agriculture and carpet-making, and their way of life is very primitive and close to the soil.

It is known for certain that the Caucasians learned the art of knotting carpets from the Turkomans, and they brought this to its highest perfection under the Persians, though they always remained faithful to their own individual style. In their absolutely geometrical patterns we find the ruggedness of the overhanging rocks, the harshness of the ice-capped peaks, the deep valleys of their country; in the bold colour-contrasts we find their native genius and a desire to resist outside influences and live their own life. The patterns are abstract and symbolic, and mysterious and ingenuous at the same time; they arouse the same interest as all primitive things which contain in them the clues to human expression and creation. Caucasian carpets are all worked entirely in wool, warp and weft both included, and made with Ghiordes knots. They are almost always small and rather elongated and many of them are prayer-rugs.

On a single-coloured background, generally red or blue, the vivid decoration stands out, arranged with a symmetry more apparent than real because it is determined by instinct and improvisation. Signs and symbols are many and varied; we find the eight-pointed star of the Medes, the six-pointed one of the Mahomedans, the triangle, the square, the hexagon, the Greek cross, the hour-glass, the comb, the dagger, the hook (said to be a derivation of the swastika) and here and there a few highly stylised flowers. The whole is clearly outlined with a very exact edging, which takes the place of shading. Figures of people or animals, also highly stylised, are found more often in carpets from the southern districts, the commonest being those of the crab, tortoise, camel, dog, peacock, tarantula and eagle. A frequent pattern in the borders is a design notched on both sides, alternating with a kind of cup, which is said to represent the lotus-flower in water. Other border patterns are composed from Kufic writing, and there is also one known as the 'running dogs', which is like a long row of hooks.

At first sight these designs might seem to be some-what childish in their simplicity, but they are, in fact, the fruits of centuries of struggle against man and nature. In the bright and brilliant colours we read the story of man's aspirations to a joy which life denies, or, if it allows it, then it is only at the cost of immense sacrifice. We see there a jealous, resolute individual-ism and the proof that earnestly sought happiness not yet achieved is the deepest feeling man can know.

Armenian carpets (so-called). These are ancient carpets whose origins are somewhat uncertain. The centre of production is Armenia, a region to the south of the Caucasus, north of Persia and situated on the roads to Turkestan, Asia Minor and the West. This is the source of the many influences shown in the decora-tion, which is decidedly Mongol as well as Persian in inspiration. These characteristics were assimilated by the Armenian carpet-makers to such an extent that they gave rise to an altogether individual style of their own. The basic motif is the dragon (or the phoenix in combat with the dragon) and is so stylised that it looks like long jagged leaves arranged like a trellis. Other animals are also portrayed, but it is difficult to identify them without knowing their origin and significance. Generally they form very elegant patterns, distinguished by their deep and restful colours. They are very skilfully worked with finest quality wool. Almost impossible to find nowadays, they are in great demand by collectors.

Daghestan. Daghestan means 'country among the mountains' and is an eastern province of the Caucasus, situated on the shores of the Caspian Sea, with its northern slopes bordering on the Russian steppe. The region is furrowed with gorges and overhanging cliffs, in the midst of which are luxuriant tablelands with a wealth of pasturage well suited to the rearing of sheep and camels. The people, who live in separate tribes, come from the most aristocratic Caucasian stock as is evident in their carpets.

Their geometric design gives the impression of a mosaic enclosed in differently coloured bands arranged diagonally. They are finely knotted, with a really exceptional harmony of colouring, and are among the most ancient of Caucasian carpets. Even modern specimens retain certain traditional features, but the ancient carpets are now impossible to come by, since they were made to be kept and handed down from generation to generation as family property.

Derbent. Derbent, the most important city of the Daghestan district, situated on the shores of the Caspian Sea, was for many years a Persian military outpost, placed there as a safeguard against northern invasions. It is an important assembly point and market for the carpets produced in the neighbourhood. The makers of Derbent carpets come of Tartar stock, which explains why their work is coarser, heavier and rougher than that of Daghestan. They have the same thick pile, dense and glossy, as Kazak carpets, and their strongly accentuated geometric designs are separated from each other by broad bands in plain shades. The colours, always vivid, are usually red, blue and yellow, and give the carpet a certain savage and primitive aspect.

Karabagh. Karabagh is the southernmost province of the Caucasus and, because it is nearest to Persia, is the district that has always been most influenced by that country. Karabagh carpets have an unusual and curious ornamentation; they are almost always long carpets, with very bright and vivid colours. One circumstance which has left its mark strongly on Karabagh designs is the fact that carpet-makers from this district were invited to France in the 18th century to make Savonnerie carpets. Hence the decidedly French flavour of the ornamentation.

Kazak. In the Erivan district of the southern Caucasus, dominated by the view of the Biblical Mount Ararat, live the nomadic Kazak tribes, whose origins are not known. The name Kazak clearly derives from Cossack, and it has been established that their origins go back to the Russian Cossacks, and that they are probably the result of some invasion. An independent, intelligent and proud people, with many points in common with the Turkomans, they consist largely of shepherds, daredevil horsemen and brigands. They are a people who never build houses, since they live in caves or under canvas, and according to the season they wander between the plains and the mountains.

Kazak carpets reflect the strength and independence of these people. They differ from all other Caucasian carpets in their widely spaced geometrical decoration: against a very open, single-coloured background, polygons of various shapes stand out boldly, surrounded by familiar Caucasian patterns. The rich and vivid colours are deliberately arranged to clash, and reds, blues and greens are dotted with yellow and white. They have a deep and glossy pile, and their shape is that of a rectangle which is almost a square. Their whole effect is unmistakably Oriental.

Seichur. In the Daghestan district, south of Derbent and north of Kuba, lies the village of Seichur, where at one time typically Caucasian carpets were produced. It can be said that these were early models which were the originals of many kinds of south Caucasian carpet, better known today than the

Seichur carpets, which have now almost completely disappeared.

Distinguishing features are their fine colouring, patterns less rigid than those of other Caucasian carpets, the 'Greek cross' and the white border, with its widely spaced 'running dog' design.

Shirvan, Kabistan and Kuba. The homeland of Shirvan carpets lies in the southern part of Daghestan, from which it is separated by the Caucasus mountains, and it extends as far as the shores of the Caspian Sea. It is a region subject to continual demands for carpets, and consequently it is feared that the type produced there may become standardised. At present they are really gay and attractive carpets which have many Daghestan features, with some Persian influence as well in the floral design of the borders, though these are always stylised. Sometimes these carpets have both warp and weft in cotton, instead of wool as is usual for Caucasian carpets. The pile is close-cut, and the carpets are finely knotted, thin and easy to handle.

The same may be said of Kabistan carpets, made in the Kuba district. They are artistic and refined carpets, always long and narrow and extremely carefully worked. Those from Kuba, a small city to the south of Derbent, belong to this same group. Their distinguishing characteristic is the Kufic writing in their borders and the ever recurring motifs of the hook-shaped leaf and the dagger. They are quietly elegant.

The prayer-rug in all these types generally has white or brown as its background colour.

Soumak. The Soumak carpet derives directly from Kilims and is made by nomadic tribes in the southern Caucasus. If its designs belong unmistakably to the group of carpets from this district, its workmanship points to Kashmir origins. It is not knotted but is worked with a needle; and while its right side has a surface as smooth as cloth, its reverse is a hotch-potch of loose ends. The designs consist of fairly large rhomboids on a background full of stars, flowers and human and animal figures, with the same stylisation that we find in Caucasian carpets. The borders always have the 'running dog' motif. Soumak carpets are invariably gay and attractive, and the beauty of their colours and their inventive composition mark them as 'artists' carpets'.

Chichi. In the north-west of Daghestan a tribe of nomad hill-dwellers make carpets of the finest craftsmanship and very intricate design. They can be recognised by their borders, whose central bands have the characteristic feature of small sticks in diagonal rows, as well as by their dark backgrounds, on which small patterns are endlessly repeated—the rosette, the diamond, the palmette. They are meticulously made and unmistakable, and are very much sought after by collectors since they belong to a disappearing craft.

CENTRAL ASIA

Central Asian carpets come from the Turkestan district known in ancient times as 'Turan', which means 'land of the shadows'. This is perhaps the description which best suits the cruel and primitive life of the inhabitants of this part of the world, cradle of the hand-knotted carpet.

The Turkoman line, which was joined by a Mongol group, gave rise to numerous tribes, of which the first and most historically important is the Salor. These people, in their endless wanderings a thousand years before the Christian era, reached from the north of Kashgar as far as Samarkand and Merv, where the Mongol tribes settled and abandoned the nomad life. The Turkomans, however, carried on their wild and independent existence, devoting themselves to hunting and robbery, living in caves or in their tents, which were raised on osier trellises and hauled about on primitive wagons. Their precept, 'It is futile to build palaces, castles and cities, since in the end they will be only ruins', checked their thoughts of any permanent way of life. However, the need for shelter from the cold and the weather drove them to try to improve the strength and durability of the mats made from vegetable fibre decorated with threads of interwoven wool which were all they had for walls, floor and bedding. This was the origin of true knotting, which gives a special depth and firmness to the fabric. From then onwards, their tents and caves were literally lined with carpets, which sheltered them from both heat and cold. Wars, invasions and continuous migrations brought the Turkomans into contact with other peoples, who learned from them the art of knotting. However, while the other Oriental peoples raised this new type of textile to the level of a real work of art, the Turkomans still adhered to a set scheme, with few variations of pattern and colour. What is amazing is their combined achievement of magnificent craftsmanship with the special quality of their wool, as well as their special and inimitable shade of red. This they kept strictly secret, as the Chinese did with their yellow, the Persians with their blue and the people of Pompeii with their red, so it could never be rivalled by others. The great cities of Kashgar, Samarkand, Bokhara and Merv had in the meantime attained a high level of civilisation. Accepting the Mahomedan religion the population, consisting of Mongols, Tartars and some Turkomans, also adopted an advanced way of life. Schools of poetry and philosophy, miniature painting and weaving flourished, bringing daily life to a high artistic level. All was swept away when Genghis Khan arrived from Mongolia to conquer Persia.

Tamberlaine, installed at Samarkand in the late 14th century, seemed with the splendour of his court to bring life back to the district, but his cruelty, combined with his complete intolerance of the demands of the Turkomans, gave no positive support to any revival. And so this country which had once been fertile became the inevitable highway of the armies of the various surrounding peoples.

To make things even worse there were also outbreaks of small-scale guerrilla warfare and internal raids between the different tribes, who in their turn fought for themselves and for survival.

Meanwhile, to meet life's needs, carpets continued to be made; but by now love and personal interest in them had come to an end and the Turkoman carpet stuck rigidly to an established pattern. Since then the basic colour has always been red, in all its shades, unvarying and continuous. Against this, geometric patterns stand out in ivory, outlined in brown, with a rare touch here and there of dark blue, yellow, light blue and, very occasionally, green. There is endless repetition of the 'rose of Salor', the 'camel's foot' or 'elephant's foot', the trefoil, the arrows, the sticks and the diamond. The 'camel's foot', the 'elephant's foot' and the 'rose of Salor' are all differently shaped octagons, divided in various ways crosswise into four parts, arranged in parallel and perpendicular rows. This monotony of composition did not impair the charm of the ancient carpets: in fact it seemed to express the endless movement of this determined and restless people. But now it is merely a dead formula, revealing poverty of creative imagination, and showing to what an extent these people have remained fixed in their primitive way of life. Turkoman carpets, generally known by the name of the chief and best known centre in Turkestan, Bokhara, are worked entirely in wool (surfaces, warp and weft) and comprise a wide range of quality and size. Typical Turkoman carpets are the 'saddlebags', that is to say small carpets made in the shape of a bag to hang from a horse or inside a tent and used to store tools and clothing. 'Saddlebags', like the other carpets, are sometimes fine and sometimes rough. Side by side with large carpets, so carefully made that they might be thought the handiwork of a king, are found small, badly made carpets, clumsy, dull coloured and lacking in all originality. This resembles the history of Turkestan which, because of the split between nomads and settled peoples, sees one part of its population striving to attain a high level of civilisation and a way of life with artistic ideals, and the other part struggling for its very existence and freedom, and so remaining helpless children of nature.

Afghan and Baluchistan. Afghan carpets, woven in Afghanistan, which lies to the south of Turkestan, come under the heading of Turkoman carpets. Their unmistakable feature is their dark red background on which large octagons or hexagons are arranged, outlined in brown and divided crosswise in four parts in parallel perpendicular rows; each part contains geometric patterns in ivory or apricot. They are woven in coarse goats', sheep's or camel's wool, with warp and weft sometimes in wool and sometimes in cotton, and their knotting is rather clumsy. They are usually large, but small prayer-rugs and saddlebags are also to be found. The modern carpets are almost always chemically treated and have softer colours, but they remain of little value.

Similar to these, though inferior in quality, are

the Baluchistan carpets, made in the district of that name south-west of Turkestan. They are worked for the most part in dark colours by nomadic tribes leading a primitive life, and this is faithfully reflected in the colouring of the carpets—dark red, dark blue and a few touches of ivory-white. Small carpets are preferred and are altogether without originality or invention, drab and lifeless like the region from which they come.

Beshir. These carpets are produced in the district which lies on the banks of the river Oxus, to the north of the Afghan frontier. They have distinct Turkoman features and always adhere in every detail to a fixed pattern. On a deep red background, a stylised floral pattern unwinds endlessly and symmetrically, with yellow as its main colour, and a few touches of blue and green. Beshir carpets are always well made and elegant and belong to a class of carpet now disappearing.

Bokhara or Tekke, Hachly and Pendik. Bokhara is a generic term generally used to describe the whole output of Turkestan, both ancient and modern. But the name is specific and refers to the province of Bokhara for ancient carpets and to the city of the same name for modern carpets. Today, the city is part of the Turkoman Soviet. In the past it was the production, assembly and marketing centre for the whole of Turkestan. Tekke is the name of a tribe which, together with the even more ancient Salor tribe,

49. Example of Shirvan carpet. 19th century (Caucasus). Private collection, Milan.

50. Example of Shirvan carpet. 19th century (Caucasus).
Private collection, Varese.

51. Shirvan Talish carpet. 19th century (Caucasus). Private collection, Milan.

53. Kuba carpet. 19th century (Caucasus). Private collection, Milan.

54. Soumak carpet, with outer border known as 'running dogs'. 19th century (Caucasus). Private collection, Milan.

55. Chichi carpet. 19th century (Caucasus). Private collection, Milan.

56. Afghan carpet (detail). 19th century (Turkestan). Private collection, Milan.

57. Beshir carpet. 19th century (Turkestan). Private collection, Milan.

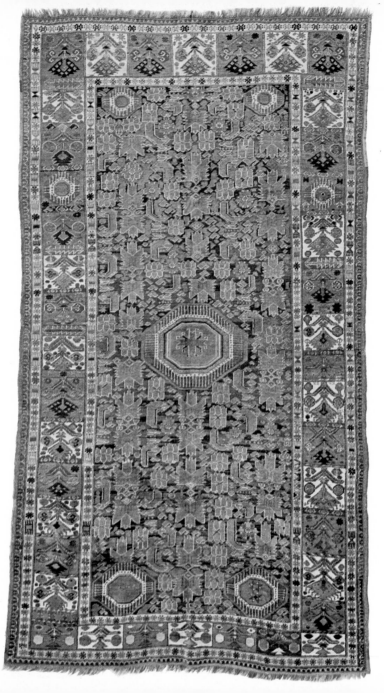

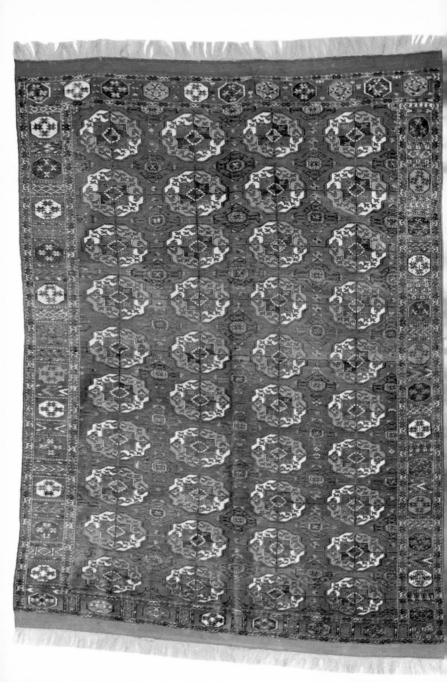

58. Bokhara carpet. 19th century (Turkestan).
Private collection, Milan.

59. Hachly carpet. 19th century (Turkestan). Private collection,
Milan.

60. Chinese carpet, with recurring cloud motiv. 19th century.
Private collection, Milan.

61. Chinese carpet with figures, scenes of everyday life outdoors. End of 19th century. Private collection, Milan.

62. Samarkand carpet, with rectangular medallions and symbolic designs. 18th century (Mongolia). Private collection, Milan.

63. Samarkand carpet, showing ancient pomegranate motif.
19th century (Mongolia). Private collection, Milan.

64. Agra carpet, with motifs derived from Persia. 19th century (India). Private collection, Milan.

created the finest Turkoman work, outstanding both in craftsmanship and the quality of its wools and patterns. They are always accurately knotted carpets, worked entirely in the finest wool; firm and closely

CHINA

The Chinese carpet-producing provinces are the northerly ones, and the main centres are at Peking, shorn, they illustrate the characteristic design which has served as a model for all subsequent Turkestan types. Octagons, arranged in perpendicular and parallel rows, stand out against a background which is always dark wine-red, almost mahogany.

This same group also includes Hachly carpets, which are mostly prayer-rugs with their main ground subdivided crosswise into four parts and which never have polygons like Bokhara designs. They are very rare and of the finest quality. Superior to all Turkestan types are Pendik carpets, whose delicate workmanship is done in silk as well as the finest wool. They are always small, soft and velvety, and seldom come on to the market.

Yomud. The district of this name, which lies to the north of Khorassan and west of Bokhara, is inhabited by nomadic tribes who live on the shores of the Caspian Sea. They make carpets very like those of the Bokhara shade and is sometimes almost maroon. different in design. This consists of a pattern of hooked diamonds, which stands out in blue and ivory against a red background; it is a darker red than Bokhara shade and is sometimes almost maroon. The borders of Yomud carpets have geometrical figures in twisted rows, always in the same colours; they are well made and entirely of good quality wool. Tientsin and Ning-hsai, and in Tibet, Mongolia and Eastern Turkestan. There are no regional differences of design or workmanship and the Senneh knot is always used, with warp and weft in cotton and surfaces in wool or silk. This is because for thousands of years China has always been a united country under one single rule, without tribal subdivisions or infiltrations by other races. Hence the unity of thought of this great people, and its perfect mastery of the symbolism which pervades all its arts and crafts. From bronzes to ceramics and porcelain, from ivories to stone carving, from painting to sculpture in wood, the same symbols are always used for decoration; they always have the same meaning and are found in fabrics and carpets too. They are symbols of the teachings of China's two great masters, Confucius and Lao-tse, and to these were later added Buddhist symbols.

In the 12th century the Mahomedans brought Islamic motifs into China, but they did not have a lasting influence on the design of Chinese carpets. Indeed it was the Mahomedans who acquired certain Chinese themes, like the *Tsi,* the cloud, the swastika and others which frequently recur in Persian and Turkish carpets. Early Chinese carpets can be discussed only from the evidence of paintings and poetic descriptions. Later examples can be studied 'from life' from the Ming period (1368–1644), when they still have the ancient geometric decoration, and on through the Ch'ien L'ung period (1736–1795), which produced the finest and most sumptuous of all Chinese carpets, rich in floral decoration, with animals, houses, landscapes and figures too.

We can go as far as considering examples from the next period down to the middle of the 19th century, but no further than that unless we want to be confronted by cross-bred mass-production, aimed at a particular kind of Western bad taste. For it was then that Chinese carpets began to be in great demand from Western traders, English above all, who ordered them in bulk in sizes suited to European living conditions and choosing at random the easiest and most comprehensible designs, with neutral and unexceptionable colours. The first years of the 20th century, still in response to English demands, saw the advent of so-called 'sets', three carpets for bedroom use, which are a European idea and have nothing to do with true Chinese carpets. Thus the significance of this unique symbolism was lost.

Few people are aware today that the dragon, used as long ago as 200 BC, represents God, nature and the Emperor, and that in Chinese mythology it personifies all the powers of heaven and earth because it symbolises 'the mystery of the whole world'. Sometimes the dragon holds in his claws a pearl surmounted by a tongue of fire, which represents thunder and lightning. No one knows now that the phoenix is the symbol of the Empress and the wives, that when it is represented in five colours they signify the five cardinal virtues, and that together the phoenix and dragon symbolise happiness. No one imagines that the lion is a kindly beast, upholding the laws and protecting sacred buildings; that a sub-species of the lion is the *Fu,* or blessed dog, who guards the doors of houses and temples and protects them from the evil spirit. Likewise no one now remembers the meaning of the basic colours of Chinese carpets—blue for heaven, yellow for earth, red for the sun and white for the moon. And again the floral symbols for the four seasons—the narcissus for winter, peach-blossom for spring, and lotus (also the symbol for purity, immortality and rebirth) for summer and the chrysanthemum for autumn.

Of the many other motifs used for decorating Chinese carpets, and which it is impossible to list here, even approximately, the chief ones must not be overlooked: the swastika, or crooked cross (the Greek key-pattern derives directly from this) which represents the movement of the earth on its axis; the pomegranate, which signifies fertility; the bat, symbol of good luck; the cloud, representing immortality; the eternal knot, the butterfly, the shell, the horse, the bamboo, the rose, the lotus-flower, etc. And there are also everyday objects—the tambourine, the chessboard, paintbrushes, etc. Then there are landscapes, figures and flowers in profusion. Always with special meanings, for the most part kindly and well wishing, to complete the picture which each carpet embodies and in which each carpet expresses a special wish, according to the events and feelings that inspired it.

In conclusion, the Ming and Ch'ien L'ung periods are the most important in the history of Chinese carpets, because they produced the examples which were truest to the medium and above all to the thought of this great Asiatic people, who considered the carpet, in all its aspects, as the emblem of eternity and who called the design which decorated it 'the changing world of nature'.

SAMARKAND

These are the carpets made in the vast territory situated between China and Turkestan, which takes its name from the ancient and glorious Turkoman capital. It is a region inhabited by Chinese, Mongols, Turks, Aryans and Tibetans, and for more than 2000 years it belonged to China; its carpets confirm this by their adherence to Chinese models, from which they differ only in their rather loose knotting, in the more geometric tendency of the designs and in their shape, which is almost always elongated. Main decorative features are the square medallions, the pomegranate motifs, the tree of life, the swastika, butterflies and clouds. The most commonly used colours, incomparably beautiful, are yellow, blue and crimson-lake. Ancient Samarkand carpets still exist which deserve a place in the world's greatest museums, but modern ones are very second-rate. In the early years of the 20th century it became customary to use chemical rinses, including aniline, to brighten the colours; eventually this had a damaging effect on the carpet's durability, and thus it came to lose its original character.

INDIA

The beginnings of the history of the carpet in India are a little uncertain, but according to the usual accounts we can place them at the time of the Mahomedan invasion, AD 712. Even if the Indians already knew and used cloth on the floor it has been confirmed that they learned the art of knotting from the Persians; and, under the guidance of such expert masters, in the course of time they made it a highly refined art, worthy in every possible way of their other artistic achievements. As far as its mighty past is concerned, India always remains 'mysterious', since certain of her inestimable treasures, which include all the arts, painting, sculpture, architecture, jewellery, fabrics etc., are known to us only from reading eye-witness accounts. The same can be said of the legendary carpets known to have adorned the palaces of princes, a few of which, perhaps, still exist secretly in some ancient family homes. These examples belong to the golden age of the Indian carpet, that is to say to the time of the Mogul dynasty, which began with Babur's defeat of the Indian army in 1526. Akbar (reigned 1556–1605), Babur's grandson, was the greatest of the Moguls, giving such impetus to all forms of art and thought in his country that he is often compared to Shah Abbas the Great of Persia. During his reign, India achieved splendours never before dreamed of, and contemporary witnesses describe unimaginable carpets and other treasures.

Akbar, imitated by all the princes who were subject to him, created a great carpet-making industry and invited Persian artists and craftsmen to his court. This explains why Indian carpets are made with very fine Senneh knotting, both warp and weft being in cotton, and the decoration performed in a decidedly floral style.

Indian silk carpets were particularly exquisite, and are described as being far superior to all Persian work.

The main carpet-making cities were Agra, Fathpur and Lahore, and these were joined in the 17th century by New Delhi.

At this time the Portuguese, the Dutch and above all the English had already begun to trade with India; consequently carpet-making began to be an industry aimed at the European market, and thus it lost its main Indian characteristics.

In 1738 the Persian Shah Nadir overcame the resistance of Aurungzeb, the last of the Moguls, and took him prisoner. Nadir sowed death and destruction everywhere, took possession of the famous 'Peacock Throne' and returned to Persia, leaving

India completely impoverished and a prey to new conquerors, who from then on succeeded each other until India was made an English colony.

CONCLUSION

Today the output of Indian carpets is, after Persian, perhaps the most numerous and widespread in the world. Designs are worked in the French style, to such an extent that they are called 'Indian Savonneries' and, when they are not knotted but worked with a needle, 'Indian Aubussons'. These last are generally made in Kashmir, the region once called 'the garden of eternal spring', and where in the 17th century the finest and most harmonious royal carpets were made.

An enormous carpet-making industry is engaged on copying Chinese designs, not to mention the influx of carpets from Pakistan. This produces copies of all types of carpet, especially those from Bokhara, done in crude colours (by means of aniline dyes) which no one in Turkestan ever dreamed of. Both warp and weft are invariably in cotton, instead of being in wool as is usual for Bokhara work, so these carpets are only bad copies of the originals. An avalanche of carpets pours into every country of the world, above all America and South Africa, and this, if it were to cease, would bring unemployment to a large part of the population of India. This new industry, altogether lacking in artistic taste and tradition, has nevertheless preserved at least one of the Indian talents—the outstanding manual skill which still achieves precise and minute knotting, perfection of pattern and rare mastery of workmanship. There is truth in the ancient Indian saying: 'The first, best and most perfect tool is the hand of man.'

LIST OF ILLUSTRATIONS

1.   Ancient Ushak carpet, known as 'the Holbein' or 'painters' carpet'. 16th century (Asia Minor). Bardini Museum, Florence. Highly decorative in its elegant yellow arabesque, which unfolds on the red background—the same arabesque often found portrayed in the pictures of Renaissance painters.

2.   Ladik. 17th century (Asia Minor). Bardini Museum, Florence. Prayer-rug, characteristic with its three niches, separated by columns, which represent the entrance to the temple. These are topped by a section featuring 'Rhodes lilies'. Note the colour effects, discreetly balanced against the unusual yellow background.

3.   Ancient Persian hunting-scene carpet (detail). 16th century. Poldi Pezzoli Museum, Milan. An inscription in the central medallion gives the maker's signature and the date— 929 of the Hegira, which corresponds to AD 1523. Admirable for the mastery with which human and animal figures are portrayed.

4.   Ancient Persian carpet with inscriptions. 16th century. Poldi Pezzoli Museum, Milan. In the narrow inside border Persian legends are inscribed, giving poetic accounts of the naturalistic féatures which compose the carpet's decoration.

5.   Ancient carpet from Tabriz. First half of 16th century (Persia). Musée des Arts Décoratifs, Paris (Gift of J. Maciet). With free and lively fantasy, the artist evokes a whole world of fable here. Animals alternate with flowers and birds in a fluid and mobile composition. Warp and weft are in cotton, and the colours, particularly vivid, are obtained from natural vegetable dyes.

6.   Ancient Tabriz carpet (detail). First half of 16th century. Musée des Arts Décoratifs, Paris. Here again flowers, birds and even a waterfall and a mythical animal in an increasingly close and rhythmical pattern make this a real masterpiece.

7.   Ardebil carpet with inscriptions, signature and the date 946 (AD 1539). Victoria and Albert Museum, London. Believed to be the oldest in existence before the carpet in the Poldi Pezzoli Museum was made known. This ancient Persian carpet is called Ardebil because until the 20th century it covered the venerated tomb of Sheikh Ssefi, founder of the Safavid dynasty, which came from Ardebil.

8.   Ancient hunting-scene carpet (detail). 16th century (northern Persia). Musée des Arts Décoratifs, Paris. Animal figures and vegetation are used side by side in a free and spacious pattern although here there is more stylisation than in the comparable carpet from Tabriz. This stylisation is emphasised by floral decorations.

9.   Fragment of an ancient Persian carpet, said to be 'Polish', perhaps because the carpets were made at the behest of Polish princely families. Kunstgewerbemuseum, Vienna. Here the ornamentation is particularly interesting as it is decidedly close to that of Armenian carpets.

10.   Carpet with medallions (detail). 16th century (Persia). Victoria and Albert Museum, London. The medallion is a characteristic Persian decoration and gives carpets a charm altogether foreign to those from the Caucasus or Anatolia. In the free and fluid ornamentation of medallion carpets the Persian spirit expresses itself in all its joyful spontaneity.

11.   Ancient Persian carpet. 17th century. Kunstgewerbemuseum, Vienna. This belongs to the collection known as 'the Shahs' carpets' but is usually called 'Polish'.

12.   Bakhtiari. 19th century (Persia). Private collection, Milan. Carpet with natural camel-wool background, on which can be seen the stylised floral decoration; the geometrical medallions do much to accentuate its ingénuous, primitive character.

13.   Bijar. 19th century (Persia). Private collection, Milan. Carpet on whose background of light blue (a colour seldom to be found in these works) strongly marked Persian motifs stand out. Strong and hard-wearing, these carpets are suited to many different uses.

14.   Feraghan. 19th century (Persia). Private collection, Milan. In this carpet can be seen all the characteristic motifs of the Feraghan region against the fine red background that is an especially distinguishing feature. The recurrence of the palmette motif is typical.

15. Naim. 20th century (Persia). Private collection, Milan. An example of recent Iranian work, filling in the usual medallion pattern with small floral designs. Decidedly one of the better recent carpets.

16. Hamadan (detail). 19th century (Persia). Private collection, Milan. Carpet worked in natural-coloured camel-wool. Both its long and narrow shape and the geometrical medallions, with their thick decoration, are typical of the region.

17. Heriz (detail). 19th century (Persia). Private collection, Milan. Carpet with geometric patterns well spaced on light backgrounds. This is an example of a characteristic type in marked contrast to the traditional Persian genre.

18. Ancient Herat carpet (detail). 17th century (Persia). Bardini Museum, Florence. All the characteristic features of Herat carpets can be seen here in harmonious elegance, standing out from the wine-red background and the fine green of the border. Accurately and closely knotted.

19. Karaja (detail). 19th century. Private collection, Milan. The nearness of this region to the Caucasus results in a decisive influence on design and colouring.

20. Ispahan (detail). 19th century (Persia). Private collection, Milan. Among the best Persian carpets and of very fine workmanship, Ispahan specimens feature close knotting and exactness of design. Here can be seen the repeated representation of a hand which grasps the phoenix, symbol of happiness.

21. Kashan. 19th century (Persia). Private collection, Milan. This carpet, too, is among the best Persian examples, with its typical pattern of little flowers filling both the centre and the rich borders. The knotting is finely done, and the wool soft and silky.

22. Kirman carpet. 19th century (Persia). Private collection, Milan. Kirman, which lies on the Iranian tableland, was at one time called 'the rose-garden of Persia'. Towards the 18th century the makers of these carpets won great renown and prestige for their colours and designs, which were indeed remarkable. At Kirman, Persian decorative fantasy reached complete fulfilment in all its gracefulness and exquisite courtliness.

23. Khorassan (detail). 19th century (Persia). Private collection, Milan. Typical carpet from this district, with its continual repetition of the palmette and rosette themes, both in the three medallions and in the two panels with their light backgrounds.

24. Meshed. 19th century (Persia). Private collection, Milan. Although not of the finest workmanship, this is nevertheless an unusual carpet in the elegance of its design and colours. Note the rich inner border with the palmette transformed into a highly decorative feature.

25. Saruk. 19th century (Persia). Private collection, Milan. A characteristic example of this type, following the tradition from which it has never departed. In this particular specimen note the pleasing colour effect, unusual in a Saruk carpet.

26. Shiraz. 19th century (Persia). Private collection, Milan. An excellent example of the old carpets from this region. The high qualities of design and workmanship seen here have vanished from modern carpets.

27.   Senneh. 19th century (Persia). Private collection, Milan. An exceptional and delicate example of this very special type, among the finest Persian carpets and noted for its close knotting and softness. The pattern includes the inevitable palmette and rosette but unlike the usual Senneh designs has figures of various animals at the centre.

28.   Serabend Mir (detail). 19th century (Persia). Private collection, Milan. A carpet preserving its character unchanged, both in the main pattern, which endlessly repeats the palmette, and in the elegant borders. It never departs from the old proto-types.

29.   Teheran. 20th century (Persia). Private collection, Milan. Though produced recently, this is a carpet which keeps to the old patterns, repeating them with careful workmanship and sober colours. Nevertheless they are of poor quality.

30.   Tabriz (detail). 19th century. Private collection, Milan. This carpet can be recognised by the large central medallion, which stands out on a plain background and is repeated, quartered, at the corners. In its better features it follows the classic conventions of Persian work.

31.   Caesarea or Panderman. 19th century (Asia Minor). Private collection, Milan. Prayer-rug with the lamp at the centre of the niche and surrounded by carnations, among the region's favourite flowers. It belongs to the old tradition and maintains the best standards.

32.   Syrian or Damascan carpet from the court workshop. 16th century. Pogliaghi Collection, Varese. Like all carpets from this district and period it is worked in red, green and turquoise, with accurate Islamic geometric decorations.

33.   Ghiordes. 18th century (Asia Minor). Private collection, Milan. Ancient prayer-rug, representing the mythical 'seven heavens of Allah' in its borders; the niche is green, a colour seldom used as a background because it is featured in Mahomed's banner and therefore considered sacred.

34. Bassra Ghiordes. 17th century (Asia Minor). Private collection, Milan. Belonging to a group which has now disappeared, this carpet is typical in its use of cotton outlining in white the rich, elegant and refined ornamentation.

35. Hereke. 18th century (Asia Minor). Private collection, Milan. Prayer-rug with numerous inscriptions from the Koran, with ciphers completing the ornamental composition. Among these note the 'Tsi', which was Chinese in origin.

36. Kirshir (detail). 18th century (Asia Minor). Private collection, Milan. Elongated carpet with geometrical medallions aligned on a spacious ground. It displays colours typical of this region: bright red, green verging on yellow and touches of white to add freshness.

37. Kula. 18th century (Asia Minor). Private collection, Milan. Prayer-rug, with the stylised tree of life in the centre of the niche and the columns of the temple at the sides. The yellow, pea-green and blue are typical colours.

38. Melas. 18th century (Asia Minor). Private collection, Varese. This carpet is unmistakable in its floral design— which includes the ever-present carnation and the diamond— as well as its centre, formed from a rectangle on a light ground.

39. Pergamos (detail). 18th century (Asia Minor). Private collection, Milan. A rich example with no Anatolian features. Derives from the Caucasus in its design and from Turkoman work in its clear, lively and brilliant colouring.

40. Sivas. 19th century (Asia Minor). Private collection, Milan. An example of Anatolian work, which repeats Persian patterns. This carpet features the tree of life, represented in a close-packed and tiny design of delicate colours which takes up all the central space.

41. Transylvania or Siebenbürgen. 17th–18th centuries (Asia Minor). Private collection, Monza. An unusual prayer-rug made in the old days. Most of these are to be found in the churches of Transylvania and in a few rare collections.

42. So-called Armenian carpet (detail). 18th century (southern Caucasus). Private collection, Monza. Ancient example which uses Caucasian elements in the design combined with Mongol and Persian variations. The elegant yellow background colour is unmistakable.

43. Daghestan (detail). 19th century (Caucasus). Private collection, Milan. This carpet is distinguished by its consistent decoration in diagonal stripes, which repeat the palmette motif (Indian in origin and distorted in accordance with Caucasian taste) and by the remarkable harmony of its colours.

44. Derbent (detail). 19th century (Caucasus). Private collection, Milan. Example of clear-cut geometric design, well balanced, with strong and definite colours, as in primitive Caucasian work.

45. Karabagh. 19th century (Caucasus). Private collection, Milan. The ornamentation of this carpet—geometric and at the same time floral, with vivid colours—indicates that it was made somewhere near Persia; on the other hand the spacious lay-out of the centre, with its plain background, is typical of the Caucasus and, more precisely, of Kazak.

46. Seichur. 19th century (Caucasus). Private collection, Milan. The geometric design of these carpets is less stylised than the foregoing. Characteristics are the representation of the Greek (St George's) cross in the central pattern and the 'running dogs' motif in the outer border.

47. Kazak. 19th century (Caucasus). Private collection, Varese. The two large designs which occur in the central field of the carpet are found exclusively in Kazak work. Some scholars think they represent 'eagles', others call them 'the swords'. In this example the colour scheme shows great artistry.

48. Kazak. 19th century (Caucasus). Private collection, Milan. The broad, geometric pattern and the strong and definite colours of this carpet are typical of work from this region. There are interesting representations of the crab, the spider and the diamond in the open central field and in the border.

49. Shirvan. 19th century (Caucasus). Private collection, Milan. A very rare example in its elegance of composition and the nobility of the colours. While it maintains the fundamental features of its type, it creates an unusually lively and refined whole.

50. Shirvan. 19th century (Caucasus). Private collection, Varese. This carpet is typical of the huge output of this region, both in shape and in its elegant and refined colouring. Note the stylisation of vases with leaves on the light ground of the border.

51. Shirvan Talish. 19th century (Caucasus). Private collection, Milan. Characteristic of these carpets is their shape, always long and narrow, and open designs. An unusual feature here is the central field, which is entirely filled with eight-pointed diamonds; Talish carpets usually have an empty central field, worked in a plain colour, generally yellow.

52. Shirvan Kabistan. 19th century (Caucasus). Private collection, Milan. This, too, is an example of the most refined Caucasian work, and is distinctive in its great accuracy of design, which includes favourite motifs from this region.

53. Kuba. 19th century (Caucasus). Private collection, Milan. A delicately designed carpet, rich in symbols and representations, among which can be seen Kufic lettering in the borders. Along the sides of the central field is the ever-recurring dagger motif.

54. Soumak. 19th century (Caucasus). Private collection, Milan. Not a knotted carpet, but one which was worked with a needle. It displays all the ornaments characteristic of the Caucasus, as well as modifications of geometric medallions, and the inevitable outer border with its so-called 'running dogs' motif.

55. Chichi. 19th century (Caucasus). Private collection, Milan. These carpets always have the finest workmanship and ornament and feature sober colours. They are distinguished by a central border with diagonally arranged motifs. Rather rare.

56. Afghan (detail). 19th century (Turkestan). Private collection, Milan. This old specimen, worked in the unmistakable shades of brown and red, has the characteristic geometric panels typical of all Turkoman work.

57. Beshir. 19th century (Turkestan). Private collection, Milan. A very elegant carpet which, while keeping to the basic colours of Turkoman carpets, breaks away from them in its ornamentation. Its central field is closely filled with intersecting motifs, among the most important of which is a sectional view of a carnation.

58. Bokhara. 19th century (Turkestan). Private collection, Milan. The classic model from which all other Turkoman types are derived. Here the panels, or polygons, are less rigid and rectangular than in Afghan carpets and thus give a softer effect.

59. Hachly. 19th century (Turkestan). Private collection, Milan. This carpet, while it repeats the colours generally used in Turkestan, is altogether different from other types from this region. It never has panels on its central field, which is always closely filled with small patterns.

60. Chinese carpet. 19th century. Private collection, Milan. There is a recurring cloud motif along the border and other symbols and ideograms in the central field; among these the example in the middle is of vital significance.

61.   Chinese carpet with figures. End of 19th century. Private collection, Milan. A scene of everyday life, the composition is full of interest because of the different attitudes of each character.

62.   Samarkand. 18th century (Mongolia). Private collection, Milan. Carpet with oblong medallions and symbolic representations, among them the vase containing the tree of life. The borders include the key-pattern, which has ancient Eastern origins.

63.   Samarkand. 19th century (Mongolia). Private collection, Milan. A rare carpet, in silk, displaying the ancient theme of the pomegranate, symbol of fertility and plenty, which grows out of a small vase and overruns the whole central field.

64.   Agra. 19th century (India). Private collection, Milan. Indian carpet with motifs of Persian derivation, but its place of origin is clearly seen in its use of blue and yellow.